*mend**ED***

a story through eating disorder recovery

WRITTEN BY ASHLEY LEKHRAM

ISBN: 9798432885159

Disclaimer: This poetry book is a memoir. It reflects my present recollections of experiences over time. Some names and characteristics have been changed, some events have been compressed, and some dialogue has been recreated.

Numbers are blacked for triggering purposes. If you are struggling and are triggered by the content in this book, look into my resources page located in the back, and reach out for help. Treatment is available. Help is available.

Edited by Logan Davis
Cover Art by Anita Mangra

For more poetry content by Ashley Lekhram, follow @writer.in.recovery on Instagram.

This book is dedicated to my Grandma Diane, who always told me I should write a book. I did it, Grandma. I did it.

I wish you were here to read this. Thank you for encouraging me to keep writing.

I miss you, my pretty lady. I hope this makes you proud.

(June 3ʳᵈ 1942 - July 23ʳᵈ 2019)

A huge shoutout and thank you to Annalisa, my admissions counselor at treatment, for being the inspiration for the title of this book.

When I was so hopeless, fighting for my treatment, you fought with me. Every step of the process, you were with me, and I couldn't be more thankful. From my very first day to my last day, 10 months later, you were with me. Thank you for helping me get the help I needed. Thank you for being more than just an admissions counselor. Thank you for being a friend. mendED would not be mendED without you (literally). I miss you and our chats under the oak tree. *Thank you for reminding me that whatever is broken can be mended.*

Trigger warning: Mention of weight loss, calories, suicidal ideation, anorexia, self-harm, body image, and trauma.

Please engage in self-care while reading.

ADMITTING THE TRUTH

I'm tired of hiding underneath loose clothes, and sharp bones
I'm tired of hiding, of lying, of shying away

I have anorexia...
I say

But it's not who I am.
It's just a part of me, god damn.

I have anorexia
And I'm tired of living with this dysania

I'm tired of hiding
I'm tired of hiding
I'm **tired** of hiding

But I'm finally free,
Can't you see?
This is my recovery.

- I don't have to lie anymore
  The truth is in these pages

breaking

She hid this for so long
She even hid it from herself,
But it's right in front of her
It's screaming at her

Collar bones and ribs so sharp
It could stab you with one touch
Stomach growls and cries
It's begging her to stop.
But she can't.
She won't.

The smell of fear.
The taste of saltiness from her tears.

It has taken over her mind.
It is consuming her body.

It's then she realizes
That the person screaming at her
Is just her reflection in the mirror.

Slip-ons and closed toed shoes

to hide the bones,

loose fit clothes

to hide the moans

Always hiding, always lying

So no one can see me

It's exhausting, putting up this invisible shield

I'm starving, I'm hiding, I'm lying

It's hectic, not poetic

I'm just anorexic.

THE DISAPPEARING ACT

I guess you could call me a magician from the way I've learned to shrink myself till you can longer see me standing in front of you. I call it the disappearing act. It's my greatest talent, but also my greatest weakness. A measuring tape wrapped around my waist; numbers plastered all over my tiny body. A crowd of people watching, anxiously awaiting the final act. Biting their fingernails, one blink of an eye, and I am gone. Crowd goes wild. Claps echo into thin air. They're amazed I could do such a thing. Little do they know, the *only amazing thing is that I'm still alive.*

- if you know, you know.

the thing about an eating disorder is that he will fight you
till your left laying on the floor, out of breath, and bruised
yet he will tell you that it was your fault
he will scream at you, tell you you're weak and broken
a lost cause
and you start to believe him
and you listen to his demands
just to get him to shut his mouth
you tell yourself that this is the last time
and that you're ready to let him go
but then he creeps his way back in
smirking as he promises you that this time will be different
you know it won't, but there's always that little voice, whispering
"what if?"
"what if this time he's right?"
"what if this time it will be different?"

so, you give him another chance
but you're left
laying on the floor
out of breath
and bruised
again.
and he told you it was your fault
again.

-     *it will never be different*

I'm so tired of putting a smile on my face
Day after day
Pretending to be okay

Pretending that the pizza I ate was just pizza
And not a monster that was going to kill me
Pretending that the number on the scale was just a number
And not a depiction of my worth
Pretending that the calories on the back of the cereal box are just
calories
And not a death sentence

It's gotten harder and harder to pretend
Because as the thoughts are circling through my mind
I begin to spiral
My hands shake, and I stare into space

My little secret is not a secret anymore
When I'm found crying on the bathroom floor
When they can see my bones, and hear my stomach groans
They start to worry, when my vision gets blurry
And I can no longer see, what's right in front of me.

- *The numbers won't kill you.*
  But the eating disorder will.

"How are you doing?" They ask.

I stopped eating / I lost five pounds / I worked out until I fainted / I slept 13 hours last night / I woke up and wished that I didn't / I cried the whole hour in therapy / I didn't look both ways when I crossed the street / I laid in bed and stared at the wall, numb / I didn't do my homework / again / I starved myself / again / I didn't call my mom last night / I stopped texting my friends / I woke up and wished that I didn't / I woke up and wished that I didn't / I woke up and wished that I didn't.

"I'm okay." I say.

how do I explain to my family and friends that I know they love me but sometimes my depression convinces me they don't. sometimes my eating disorder convinces me that the only way I will be enough is if I shrink myself. sometimes my anxiety tells me that everyone hates me and wants nothing to do with me. how do I explain to them that I can't fall asleep at night because I took too many diet pills and my heart is racing. how do I tell them that I can't get out of bed in the morning because every time I stand up I feel like I'm going to faint. how do I tell them that my stomach could be growling but I cannot get myself to eat because the thought of food makes me want to die. how do I explain to them why I cry every single night. how do I explain to them that sometimes I'll feel okay and then it all comes crashing down again. how do I explain to them that I'm trying. how do I explain to them that I'm tired of trying. I'm tired of living. ***I'm Tired Of Living Like This.***

IF MY EATING DISORDER WAS AN ABUSIVE RELATIONSHIP - PART 1

Laying on the bathroom floor, tears streaming down my face, I realize that someone is at the door. At first, it felt comforting to know that I wasn't alone. It felt comforting to know that somebody was by my side.

But he wasn't there to bring me tissues and wipe my tears. He wasn't there to bring me water, or move my hair out of my face, and tell me that I'm going to be okay. Instead, he stood over me, screaming. He screamed terrible things. He told me that I'm not enough and that I will never be enough. He told me that I'm disgusting, and no one will ever love me. He told me that I don't belong here. He told me to just disappear. He told me that the only way to feel better is to listen to him. I don't feel like I have a choice when he's standing over me, screaming in my ear. My ear starts to ring and I can no longer hear my own voice. So, I gave in. I listened.

- *I didn't feel better. I felt worse.*

I think back to that cold and dark December night. Running to the garage in tears and tripping over the beer cans scattered on the floor. I just wanted your love. I wanted you to hold me tight and tell me I was enough. I just wanted to be loved. I fought for your attention. And when I couldn't get it, I searched for it in other ways. I starved, bruised, and hurt myself until all that was left of me was scarred skin and bones. I took the pain out on myself so maybe you would just see how much love I needed. I couldn't go on much longer like this. But I didn't have it in myself to go with grace. So I didn't. I made a scene. It's all I never knew how to do. I never learned to sit with my feelings. I learned how to get up and walk away from pain, even if in the end it just caused more. That pain has taught me a lesson.

So, maybe I didn't know how to go with grace.

But I do know now that I'm allowed to take up space.

(inspired by Taylor Swift - My Tears Ricochet)

an eating disorder is an addiction.

so, believe me. I am aware of the havoc it has created in my body, in my home.

I am aware of the pain it has caused my family, the pain it has caused me.

but this is an addiction,

and I'm in too deep.

the numbers are engraved in my brain.

my behaviors create a sense of comfort.

and my routine cannot be broken,

I must weigh, starve, count, burn.

weigh, starve, count, burn.

it started out as a form of control,

but now it is controlling me.

I don't know when it began,

but I don't think it will ever end.

because I am addicted

to this addiction.

I'm angry.
I don't know who I'm angry at.
Is it me?
Is it you?
Is it God?
Is it addiction?
Or is it this f***ed up world?
Whatever it is,
I'm angry that you were taken away from me.
I don't understand why you weren't given another chance, but I was.
Sometimes, I wish I didn't get another chance.
Sometimes, I wish I could join you up there.
Wherever "there" is.
Because recovery is hard.
Now I can see why you struggled for so long.
It's not as easy as everyone says.
It's not easy to "just put the bottle down."
It's not easy to "just eat"
When the devil is screaming in your ear.
Maybe God took you away so you could be at peace.
I want to be at peace too.
I want to be with you.

REMEMBERING ANOREXIA – PART 1

I don't quite remember when I knew I had an eating disorder.
but I do remember my sister asking me why I was weighing myself
every morning, every night,
after every meal,
after using the bathroom,
after having changed my clothes multiple times
I don't remember what I said,
and I don't remember how one simple question
turned into hundreds of unanswered questions,
hundreds of lies,
and hundreds of excuses.

for so long, I felt as if these behaviors were normal.
I felt as if I was normal.
until they no longer were.
until I no longer was.
until every picture on my phone was of my body.
until I spent hours calculating calories consumed and calories burned
until my workouts ended with me lying on the floor.

it was a combination of moments
when I was no longer in control,
and my life became my eating disorder
and my eating disorder became my life.

I wake up and feel my bones,
my stomach screams and moans.
Look in the mirror, hate what I see,
my brain is screaming at me.
"Starve yourself",
it will say.
I can't go on another day.
Walk till I can't feel no more.
Run till I fall to the floor.
Lie in bed and wonder when,
when will I feel okay again?

I'm pacing around the kitchen in a panicked state
just from the thought of having to go grocery shopping
the act of eating has proven itself to be more and more difficult
the number on the scale is beginning to drop
as well as my pants size
my ribs are protruding
my bruises aren't healing
and I'm freezing
my family and friends start to worry
and I don't even know what to say
so I make excuses, smile and say I'm fine
when really, I'm dying on the inside
my body is screaming at me
my brain is screaming back
there's too many voices
too many different paths
my vision is blurry
and I can't tell which path I'm going down
is this just a part of my recovery?
Or is it another *relapse?*

AN ODE TO MY EATING DISORDER

I lay in bed and think of all the neglect, all the shame, all the pain.
My ribs are hollow, my bones protrude.
My stomach is screaming.
My mind is crying.
I'm scared.
I'm scared of everyone leaving me.
Even you, too.
You're a part of me now.
My safety blanket in times of stress.
An unhealthy coping mechanism, one might say.
But you were what I needed.
In a life full of abandonment,
you never left.

he was manipulative and charming.
he came into my life for a reason.
he saved me from drowning in the depths of the sea.
he held onto me gracefully
promised me freedom, hope, love, and light.
it felt like magic, felt like true love.
because for the first time in forever, I wasn't alone.
until I was.
alone and frozen.
sitting in the cold, begging to be loved.
I thought it was love.
turns out it was just control.
all he wanted was control.
and when he got it, it was over for me.
he was ready to kill me.
he took control of me and my kingdom and let me go.
just like that, he let me go.
I didn't know who I was without him
after all, I've been locked behind closed doors my whole life
and when he came along, he became my identity.
till all that was left of me was skin and bones.
I thought it was true love
but it was just control
in the end, he lied to me.
his name was Hans.

- I named my eating disorder Hans.

ANOREXIA VS ME

You feel like you're going to faint?
That's okay
Everything in your life is out of control
So why not control your intake?
Oh wait, you can't control me
I've taken over your life now, remember? It's all about me.
Lie to your family.
Make jokes about it so it doesn't seem so serious.
You lost weight?
Good. Now lose more.
You're an exception to the rule.
You're fine.
So keep starving yourself.
I matter more in the end. I promise you.
Everyone keeps asking why you lost so much weight.
Good, that means it's working
Your therapist wants you to get treatment, eat ■ a day?
Hell no, now lie to her too.
Everything in your life is changing
But don't worry I won't change.
I'll stay the same.
Sooner or later, I'll win this game.

numbers blacked out for triggering purposes

IT'S KIND OF LIKE JUMANJI

this disorder has turned into a sick and twisted game

a game I don't want to play anymore

I'm on my last life,

fighting to make it out alive

I don't know how to win

because every time I think I've found my way

something knocks me down again

I feel like I'm trapped in a never-ending maze

that I can't seem to get out of

I'm running in circles

retracing my path

only to find, I'm pushed back to start

should I even try to find the end?

or should I just give up instead?

my stomach is growling
it's begging me to eat

my mind is a monster
a monster I can't defeat

the voices are getting stronger
I can't keep doing this any longer

I just want to shout
GET THE F*** OUT

I don't belong here
I just want to disappear

everyone says they're so proud of me and they've seen so much growth. that I'm changing right in front of their eyes. that I'm authentic and genuine, strong and brave. a force to be reckoned with.

that's not what I see though. I don't see growth. I can feel myself shrinking with those tired and restless eyes. I feel more like a fraud. too weak, too meek, a coward perhaps. who would want to be around me?

they see me as the angel.
I see me as the devil.

if only they knew what went through my mind.

everyone says they're so proud of me
I hope one day I can be

SICK ENOUGH

the words "you're not sick enough" circle through my mind
and it fuels the eating disorder more
why do I have to "prove" my sickness in order to receive help?
please tell me, what is defined as "sick"?
is it when I'm laying in the hospital bed?
or is it when I'm six feet under?
I cry at the sight of food,
I skip meals until I can no longer feel
but yet, I'm not "sick"
because I "look great"
because my labs are great
because I haven't lost my period yet
so maybe I'm not what the media portrays as "sick"
but I'm also not what the media portrays as "healthy"
so what am I?
if you ask me, I think I am sick.
I think my sick is "sick enough"
I think my sick is valid.
I think if I have to question whether or not I'm sick enough,
then I am sick enough.

THINGS MY EATING DISORDER TOOK

my birthday // my mom's birthday // my sister's birthday // my best
friend's birthday // my sister's baby shower // downtown st pete //
nights out with my friends // field day // the birth of my nephew // my
students last day of school // family get togethers // exercising // walks
with my dog // the funeral for my best friends mom // my dogs second
birthday // easter // mother's day // taylor swift's album release // my
own room // graduating with my friends // my own classroom // pizza
// ice cream // food freedom // honesty // my personality // my life //
me.

It started with weighing myself ▮ a day
Then crying when I saw the number
Skipping breakfast
Turned into only eating a cracker for lunch
Then no lunch at all
Then only coffee to give me fuel
Then eventually no dinner
Or just a small portion on my plate
▮ calories or less,
That's all I'm allowed to consume
The voice would say
Working out turned into a daily ritual
You have to keep going until you burn ▮ calories
The voice would say
Losing weight turned into pride instead of concern
I should be proud of myself for eating
But the voice has taken over my mind
And instead
I'm proud of myself for not

numbers blacked out for potential triggers

IF MY EATING DISORDER WAS AN ABUSIVE RELATIONSHIP - PART 2

I knew I'd need to get out of it. I knew how detrimental and toxic it was to me. The bruises it left. The pain I felt. I'll just cover it up. Hide the truth. Pretend that I'm fine. But it's hurting me on the inside. Why do I feel the need to stay? It's got such a hold on me. And I can't let it go, no matter how hard I try. It's my safe haven. "At least when I have you, I won't feel so alone". My sense of comfort in this scary world. Let me just numb the pain one more time. Run away till I can't feel anything. My body screams.

Get me out of here. I don't feel safe anymore.

THE RACE

My body is in a race
A race to the finish line
But there's no end in sight
I'm constantly running
A hundred million different thoughts
A hundred million different stories
My body can't slow down
I keep running
Faster and faster
Hoping to get to that invisible finish line
But I wonder what it is at the end
Is it my recovery?
Or is it my final attempt?

mendED

I used to dream of having a giant mirror

So I could play dress up and dance and sing
And just be me
Then I turned 16
And who I was
Wasn't enough
That giant mirror turned into a game
"How many things can you notice about yourself that you hate"
I picked apart every piece of me
Sucked my stomach in till I could no longer breathe
The dressing up, dancing, and singing
Turned into crying, screaming, and manipulating
The same mirror I once loved
Became something I hated
But it didn't change
I did
Year after year, that mirror stayed the same
Year after year, I continued to change

- maybe it never was the mirror I hated, maybe it was just me

it's 1 am, and I'm still not asleep
I'm sitting here staring out into space contemplating what to do
deep down, I know, I have a lot to look forward to. I have so much to
live for.
but sometimes, it's just exhausting.
and I question if I can make it any longer. if I can do this any longer.
deep down, I know, I should be celebrating.
but sometimes, it doesn't feel right to celebrate. after all, look where
I'm at again.
deep down, I know, I have people who love and care for me. I love
and care for them too.
but sometimes, my mind gets so clouded, and it tells me that if I love
and care for them, that this would be the right thing to do.
deep down, I know, I've come so far. but sometimes, I just don't want
to go any further.
because one step back, feels like I'm back at start. but sometimes, I
just want to be at the end.

that's where I'm struggling.
because I don't know what I mean by "end".
sometimes, the end is full recovery.
and sometimes, the end is in the grave

it's all fun and games,
till he's made his way into your veins.
the mirror cracks,
and your wrists are scratched.
your stomach roars,
the pages are torn.
you're all alone,
in this place you called home.

he tells you to not be afraid,
even as your body starts to fade.
when everyone starts to worry,
you run away in a hurry,
not sure of what they'll say,
when you tell them you're not okay.

no one understands,
why I listen to his commands.
I can't tell them that I'm scared,
and that I thought he actually cared.
I'm afraid to let him go,
because I have nothing else to show.

-   *my eating disorder was all I had to show*

THE HOUSE ON THE CORNER OF THE STREET

there's a house on the corner of the street,
it's said to be haunted by ghosts of the past.
they say whoever enters, never returns.
but you don't realize it's haunted,
because of how its painted out to be.
and you won't believe its haunted,
till you're in it yourself.
it looks so inviting, so enticing,
you want to check it out, to see what the hype is all about.
so, you walk in.
the first thing you see are the haunting images,
sending you into a flashback.
then you hear their voices,
as they breathe heavily in your ear.
you try to run, but they chase you down.
they close the blinds,
shut off the lights,
and lock all the doors,
your hands are tied,
there's nowhere to hide,
you scream and shout,
but there's tape over your mouth,
and now you can't get out.

- *an eating disorder is like a haunted house*

It's a monster.
it can smell my fear.
fear fuels his anger.
he screams at me.
his voice gets louder and louder.
there's no way to tune him out.
"you're not good enough"
"you will never get better"
he leaves a bitter taste in my mouth.
he takes over my reflection,
till I can no longer see what's right in front of me.
soon, he begins to control my every move,
so that I'm no longer me,
I'm just a girl with an ED.

They told me to watch out for the monsters under the bed
But they never told me about the monsters that live inside my head
The monster who dressed as a prince
I haven't been the same ever since
He whispered words of false safety in my ear
Reminding me that there's nothing to fear
He promised royalty for me
And a chance to finally be free
He told me that beauty is pain
And I must feel it to get through the rain
His words provided comfort
Even when he pushed me to the ground, and stained me with dirt
"Beauty is pain, remember?"
So I had to surrender
I gave it all up, just to be his special prize
But all he wanted was my demise

WHEN YOUR SHADOW TAKES OVER

he's my shadow, that follows me around. I can't see him all the time, but when I do, he's big and scary. sometimes I'm aware that he's just a shadow. but sometimes he takes over my whole body and I shut down. I'm no longer there and he's no longer just a shadow. he's me. suddenly, he is controlling my every move, every thought, every decision. sometimes when he takes over, I don't even realize it. he's like a demon that has possessed me. it's like I don't realize what I'm doing until it's too late. it's terrifying, really. to suddenly lose all control of your body and mind. and I can't snap back into my true self until the damage is done. he won't leave me alone until the damage is done. I'm afraid that one day I won't ever snap back into my true self.

I'm afraid that one day he will go too far.

everyone tells me I'm so strong

but no one knows about the days I lay in bed all day, staring at the ceiling.
can't get up to shower or even eat.
the pile of laundry on my floor is screaming at me to be folded and put away.
the unopened mail labeled "important" is begging to be read.
my stomach growling, thirsting, and longing for food. something, anything.
the dirty dishes, stacked on top of one another can't wait to be cleaned.
my friends, anxiously awaiting a response from me, wondering if I'm okay.
no one knows how hard it is to simply sit up in bed and take my pill that I don't even know is working, that I don't even know if I want to take anymore. what's the point? what's the point in staying strong when as soon I start to feel even the slightest bit better, reality settles in. I'm not okay. I'm not strong. and quite honestly, I don't want to be strong.

quite honestly, I don't really want to be *here.*

I DON'T KNOW HOW TO FEEL

My body is numb
And the sweat is dripping down me
I just want this all to end
But it's hard to even imagine an end in sight
Do I stay?
Or do I go?
Do I recover?
Or do I just give it all up?
I made it this far
so I should just keep going, right?
If I did it then
I can do it now too, right?

But I don't think I want to

I'm tired
And my mind is on fire

THE DISSOCIATIVE SUBTYPE OF PTSD

I stare at my plate, begging to be ate.

The full glass of water, begging to be drank.

I hear the people around me,

Calling out my name,

But I can't move,

I can't speak.

As they speak to me, my mind screams at me.

It's an out of body experience.

My body is physically there,

But my brain is not.

Because suddenly, I'm no longer at the table,

But I'm in 10th grade, sitting alone in the cafeteria,

Staring at my plate

And that full glass of water.

-   It's not only dissociation, it's a flashback

I lied to you
I'm not okay

Healing isn't linear, you say
It's okay to fall down, you say
You're doing the best you can, you say
This is temporary, you say
In trying you're doing, you say
Mistakes are okay, you say

But that's just the thing
I am the mistake
And I'm not okay

~~But you will be one day~~

    -    in which the "you" is my therapist

mendED

I miss the days I could sit outside

And feel the rush of wind brush against me
As I watch the moon shine over the lake
And write poems
Till my fingers bleed
And my eyes run out of tears

I miss the days I could lay on my bed
And feel the warmth underneath my blankets
As I listen to the piano playing softly
And read my books
Till my head is full of a thousand different words, a thousand different stories

But most importantly
I miss the things I could do
When my mind wasn't consumed by you

-   in which the "you" is my eating disorder

MY MIND IS TOO STARVED TO BE CREATIVE

My legs are aching
My stomach is growling
My head is spinning
I can feel my body giving up
I'm exhausted
I fell down the rabbit hole far too fast
Shrank myself
Drowned in my own tears
This isn't Wonderland anymore
And I want to find my way back home

But I fell down the rabbit hole for a reason.
Home wasn't safe either.

I don't quite think you understand what I mean when I say that there is storm going on inside of my chest and I am struggling to breathe. The water rises and fills my lungs. I scream, yet no one can hear me. I'm trembling. My body is aching, my mind is racing. The clouds in my brain turn black. The thunder roars in my stomach. The lightning leaves yet another scar. The wind hits a little too hard and I'm sucked back into the water. I scream. And still, no one heard a sound. I'm alone. And I just want to go home.

But where is home?

I've cut my hair, dyed it red underneath.

I got new clothes, threw out my old ones.
I quit my job, found a new one.
I started working out, lost a few pounds.
But I'm still sitting here, staring at the TV screen, full of self-hate.
What is it gonna take for me to realize that no matter what I change
on the outside, nothing will change how I feel on the inside.
Changing my physical appearance will not change what happens when
I look in the mirror
and see a girl with
BROKEN
WEAK
CRAZY
ALONE
written all over my face with permanent marker.
It's like what my therapist once said:
you can change anything and everything about yourself,
but if you don't love yourself on the inside, nothing will change.

Everything is changing.

But the hate I feel for myself has not.

How many milligrams of Prozac or Abilify till I feel okay again?

I'M GETTING BAD AGAIN

It's getting bad again
I can't seem to put it into words
But my stomach is growling, as I'm crying in my bed
I can't find a way out of this pain.
I'm stuck and trapped in this life that feels more like a prison to me.
I'm tiptoeing around afraid I might crack.
I could crack in any minute, it's just a matter of time till I hit my
breaking point.
Slowly by slowly, I'm killing myself more.
Eating three meals a day? I can barely eat one.
Going to work without looking like a zombie?
I can barely get out of bed.
The signs are all there, but no one but me can see.
I'm not eating. Not singing. Not dancing. Not reading. Not writing.
Isolation. Loneliness. Worthlessness. Shame. Guilt.
It's eating me alive.
It's all eating me alive.
I'm walking around with these invisible scars all over me.
They won't go away, they won't heal.
They're always there, getting worse day by day.
I don't know what I'm doing anymore.
I don't know what's going on with me.
Is it withdrawal?
Or is it relapse?
Or am I just gone for good?

I DON'T CARE ABOUT YOUR DIET

how am I supposed to live without my eating disorder,
when I live in a diet cultured world
where calories are posted on every menu
where scales are sold at every store
and magazines are swearing by this new diet
I learned in recovery that my weight doesn't define me
but everywhere I go, people are talking about my weight
or their weight, or someone else's weight
and how they need to lose ▮ pounds
and how I need to gain ▮ pounds
and how they need to stop eating
and how I need to start eating
it's exhausting, really,
to be caught in this weight centered world
where food choices are ridiculed,
and appearance is valued over personality
when people truly have no idea what one is going through
so please, just stop telling me what to do
please stop commenting on my weight
and food, and exercise, and dieting
because to be honest, I hear enough from my eating disorder
I don't need to hear it from you too
I'm tired of the voices taking over
I want my own voice back
give me space so I can hear my own voice
give me space so I can recover
please, just let me recover.

THE FINAL FAREWELL TO MY EATING DISORDER

It's time for me to say farewell,
to the life you turned to hell.

Those broken ribs and scarred wrists,
are a part of me now.

But I'll recover somehow,
because this is my last farewell,
to the story you'll never be able to tell.

it's crazy how the thing that promises you the world, is the same thing that takes away your world.

mending

Chapter 1
I'm no longer just choosing recovery or anorexia.
I'm choosing life or death.

Chapter 2
I choose life. I won't let this kill me.
This isn't easy. But I will survive.

Chapter 3
Not only am I surviving, I am thriving.
I chose freedom.

I'm trying. I promise you, I am trying.

August 28, 2020

I'm driving in the car with my friends, we're blasting Taylor Swift, and for once, I feel okay. 4 hours in the car, forgetting about where the destination will take me, forgetting about where I'm headed, and where I will spend the next few months.

Before I know it, I'm in Tallahassee, stepping outside the car and unloading my bags. I say goodbye to my friends. I hold onto them tightly, my tears soaking into their shirts. I'm so thankful. 3 friends, 4 hours, one destination.

I wouldn't dare say goodbye because it's not goodbye. It's see you later.

It's see you later, recovered.

I can't promise you that it's going to get better
Or that everything will be okay
But I can promise you that it does get easier to breathe
It does get easier to put a smile on your face
And one day, you'll look both ways when crossing the street, again
One day, you can drive your car without wanting to jerk the wheel
One day, you can leave your medication on your bedside table
You can leave therapy without signing another damn safety contract
Because you won't need a safety contract
Because you will be safe in your own body
You will be safe in your own skin
So, while I can't promise you that it's all going to get better
Or that everything will be okay,
I can promise you that this sadness won't feel so debilitating
This sadness won't be written on your face
And while the sadness may still be there,
I can promise you that this sadness is not the end,
It might just be the beginning.

Dad,
This isn't fair.
We were supposed to recover together.
Go through this journey hand in hand.
But, now I'm left having to do this on my own.
Some days I wonder how the hell I can recover without you.
Some days I wonder how the hell can I *not* recover,
When that's all you've ever wanted for me.
All I hear is your voice telling me your proud of me.
And that's all I have to hold onto.
Because when I want to give up and give in,
I hold onto your eagle necklace,
And remember that you're up there soaring,
watching over me.
So, I will soar, too.
but my God, do I miss you.

mendED

126 photos of what he wants you to see
But what you don't see, is what he did to me

You don't see me crying on the bathroom floor, because I couldn't
take it anymore
You don't see me falling to the ground
From losing one too many pounds
You don't see me lying to my family
Just to protect my "fantasy"
You don't see me drowning
From all the calculating and the counting

What you see is all a lie
And it's time to say goodbye
To his little show
Time to say goodbye to those 126 photos

REMEMBERING ANOREXIA - PART 2

I don't think it's important to know how, why, or when
my eating disorder started.
I think it's more important to ask:
When did you choose recovery?
Why did you choose recovery?
And how did you choose recovery?

Again, it was never a particular moment.
It was a combination of moments,
When enough was enough.
And my life became recovery
And recovery became my life.

NOT ONE MORE

it's not easy to live in a body that is constantly fighting to stay alive. but I won't be another statistic. I will break that stigma. I will use my voice. I'm done being silent and tearing the pages in my book. knowing my story has the power to create change, then I will speak up. why should I sit back and be ashamed of myself? if shame loses its power when I share my story, then I will share. even if my voice cracks and my heart aches. not one more life will be lost to an eating disorder. not one more life will suffer. I won't be another name on a grave. I'm here now & I'm going to fight this.

- *scream it from the rooftops, I'm here now. and I'm going to fight this.*

They say recovery is possible,
but it doesn't seem that way for me.
I look to TV shows or movies,
just to feel a little free.
I'll search for anything to give me hope,
even just the slightest thing,
anything to get me by,
to see what the future can bring.

It's in small moments I realize,
that maybe I can have a future,
one I actually want,
one that doesn't seem so scary,
where the past won't haunt.

They say recovery is possible,
and that I'll be who I'm meant to be,
and while recovery may be scary,
it's something I can finally see.

if only you heard the internal monologue going on in my head; the words that come out of my mouth do not compare to the words left unsaid. I'm at war with my own thoughts. and in the end, the eating disorder gets what it wants. the voice kicks in, it's screaming at me. the future is something I can no longer see.

"starve yourself. hurt yourself. run. keep running. oh, you feel like you're going to faint? that's okay, keep running. you can't silence me today. I'm here now and I'm going to stay."

"shut up. I won't listen to you. mostly because you don't have a clue. I do belong here. and I'm going to eat. this is something I can defeat. you try to take & take & take & take. but not today. this is a decision I am going to make. I won today, and I will tomorrow too. because *I am done listening to you.*"

WHAT I LEARNED FROM FROZEN 2

when all hope is lost
and the unknown is feared
when we know for sure
that darkness has appeared
all we can do is walk towards the light
listen to that voice
and take that next step
take that next breath
and do the next right thing

My body is corrupt
My mind won't shut up
I'm lying on the floor
Wishing I wasn't here anymore
The voices are so strong
Telling me I don't belong
But I'm going to stay,
Remind myself I'll be okay.
Today, I'll get the last word,
Because my voice deserves to be heard.

THINGS THAT DON'T SUCK

my grandma's cooking. facetime calls with my family. the taste of good coffee. ordering my favorite food. watching the sunset. texting my best friends. productive therapy sessions. putting lights up in my room. my students learning something new. playing the piano. singing to my favorite song. writing a poem. watching gilmore girls. listening to taylor swift. my dogs kisses. talking to people who understand. going out with my friends. getting good grades. bath & body works candles. warm blankets. feeling the heat touch your shoulders. a baby's laugh. hearing the words "i'm so proud of you" and for once, feeling proud of myself,

too.

There are many reasons to live.

Hold onto each one. They will be there for you,
when the darkness comes.

Your favorite peach scented candle. The sky turning orange when the
sun is about to set. Running up to your mom at the airport. The taste
of your favorite coffee. The smell of your favorite coffee shop. The
feeling when your fingers hit the piano. A baby's smile when they see
your face. Seeing your favorite artist perform live. Those long hugs
when you never want to let go. Singing your favorite songs at the top
of your lungs. The sound of the ocean waves. The "i love you"s from
your best friends. The warmth of your blanket fresh out of the dryer.
The words "I'm so proud of you" coming from someone you really
love. Finishing a really good book. Writing a poem. Facetiming your
sisters. Laughing so hard your stomach hurts. Crying out all the tears
on your therapist's couch,

And how amazing it feels to get up and say,
I made it
To another day.

A LETTER TO MY BODY

I'm sorry for all I put you through (and continue to)

I know I've hurt you. Left you so tired you felt like you couldn't breathe. You didn't deserve that. I treated you the way they treated me. I took it out on you. When I look in the mirror, I don't see you. I see all my flaws. The flaws they have tattooed on my skin. But I need to remember, they're not here anymore. I am here. So next time I think about putting more pain on you, I'll begin to thank you.

Thank you for keeping me here
Through and through
(no matter what I do)

It's 1:33 am and I'm staring at my screen

I want to write
But the words don't quite spill out of me
Anymore
I want to scream
But when I open my mouth all you hear is
Silence
I don't know what is happening to me
Or maybe I do
And I just don't want to admit it
But my eyes are almost lifeless
My brittle bones are ready to crack
And I'm tired of this
I don't want to play pretend
Anymore
I want my life back
And though I know it won't be easy
I'm finally choosing
RECOVERY.

THE DIFFERENCE BETWEEN HAVE AND HAD

I have an album on my phone

I named it after my eating disorder

There is 126 photos

And it's hard to let it go.

You see, those photos don't show the reality of my eating disorder. These photos mask what it was truly like to live with this insidious disease. You see a girl smiling in the mirror, looking comfortable in her body and happy to be alive. You don't see when she was hunched over the toilet in the bathroom, tears streaming down her face, or her locking the door to her bedroom, and hiding her excessive exercise. You don't see the amount of times she stepped on the scale or logged the calories consumed and burned on that damn "health" app. You don't see when she nearly fell to the floor from feeling so dizzy, and so weak.

These photos are romanticized and glorified.

The eating disorder is romanticized and glorified.

I'm tired of hiding that truth.

If a part of rewriting my narrative means telling the truth,

then that is what I'll do.

So,

I had an album on my phone

It was named after my eating disorder

There were 126 photos

And finally, I let it go.

I know recovery is hard,
I know it is scary.
And I know you just want to stay in the eating disorder.
Because, yes, it is easier.
And yes, it is all you know.
But sometimes there's more to life than what you can see,
Think about it, you already know what it's like to live in this eating disorder.
Try and imagine what it'd be like to live beyond your eating disorder.
I guess what I'm saying is, what do you have to lose?
Your eating disorder has already taken so much from you.
Don't let it take away the possibilities of life, too.
So, just give recovery a try.
I'm not telling you to take a giant leap into recovery,
I'm asking you to take a small step.
Every day, just take one small step.
And see.

See what recovery can bring.

Recovery is a game of tug-of-war
One side being me
And the other being my eating disorder
I'm pulling the rope with all of my might
But the eating disorder pulls harder
I begin to lose grip
And I can feel myself slipping
My sneakers pushing hard into the ground
To keep me on my toes
As I'm about to give up
And let go of the rope
I feel someone behind me start tugging
And I quickly glance back to see who it is
To my surprise,
There's a whole team behind me
Fighting with me
And supporting me
While the eating disorder is on his own
And believe me, he put up a fight
He wouldn't let go
He kept tugging
But he couldn't possibly tug any other
When there's a whole team of people on my side
We continue to tug
And slowly but surely
He loses his grip,
Slides into the dirt,
Falls to the floor
And we won.

-      you are never as alone as you think you are.

AN APOLOGY TO MY BODY

I'm sorry for the times I starved you,
And for those crescent shaped scars.
All the redness I left because I went too far.

I'm sorry for leaving you exhausted,
Till you couldn't make it anymore.
And for beating you up,
Till you fell to the floor.

I'm sorry for trying to shrink you
And wanting to disappear

I'm sorry that I didn't love you
But I do need to thank you

Thank you
For keeping me
Here.

mendED

I'm sorry for hurting you,
For all those scars,
For leaving you all alone,
Till you were starved.

I'm sorry for beating you up,
Till you felt like it was the only option.
You're more than this pain,
You don't deserve this destruction

Take it easy on yourself,
You're allowed to grieve.
You're not broken,
That I truly believe.

These scars don't define you,
They're not who you are.
I won't hurt you again,
Because you're a shining star.

you buried her alive
you grabbed the shovel,
dug out a hole
and dragged her lifeless body
into the dirt,
laughing as you did.

you thought it was funny,
to bury a fragile and broken girl.

now how funny would it be,
if she rose from the grave
dirt-stained clothes,
scraped up knees and elbows,
and stood tall.
because even 6 ft under,
she found her way back

you silly girls,
she's not dead, you know?

she's alive
you didn't kill her,
I know you tried
but instead,
you gave her time to rest
you gave her space
for a new her to arise

mendED

the vase on my bedside table shattered

but the flower still bloomed
because the vase only held the flower
but the vase was not the flower

you see, my eating disorder took over my body
as my weight began to drop,
my body shattered
but I did not

because my eating disorder held me
but it was *not* me

my eating disorder tried to shatter me
and my body

but I still bloomed

mendED

My best poetry came from my darkest moments,

something about spilling the words out on paper healed me.
It brought light in, while the darkness was surrounding me.
It was then I realized,
the light wasn't in the writing
the light was in my words.
I don't need to be surrounded by darkness,
Because *I can be the light*

the happily ever after promised
did not lay in the hands of my eating disorder
in fact, it was a horror story
so, anytime I wish to go back
and reminisce on the "good days"
I'll think back to
my collar bones and ribs
that jabbed at my skin
my stomach and all the screams
all that running so fast until I couldn't breathe
it wasn't happily ever after
it was a horror story.
a horror story,
I wish to never see again.

mendED

while I look in the mirror and hate what I see,
I realize that these imperfections aren't necessarily a bad thing.

the freckles on my nose,
my overlapped teeth,
the curve of my spine,
and the scars hidden beneath.
they don't make me imperfect,
they make me, me.

I wish I could tell you I'm doing fine
But all that would be a lie
I sit on the phone for an hour
A trusted counselor asking about my life
It's scary you know,
To talk about your trauma with a stranger
Through a mobile line
It's then I realize how I'm really not okay
It'd be so easy to just hang up
Put on an act & go on with my day
But what would that do for me?
I'm here for a reason
I didn't ask for this happen
I didn't choose to suffer
Starve my way through each season
This isn't my fault
The least I can do
Is be honest
And tell the truth
Even if my voice cracks and my hands shake
I'm a little tired of drowning
In this lake
And maybe I'm not where I want to be
But at least I stayed on the line
I'm going to let that be enough

       for me

the thing about recovery
is that there is no "how-to" book
there's no equation to solve
or rule to follow
there's no report card at the end
telling you how well you did
there's no "pass" or "fail"
there's no "A" "B" "C" "D"
all your hard work is not recognized
by a trophy, certificate, sticker, gold star, or a note on the fridge
recovery isn't a test
it's not something you can memorize
rush through
or even cheat on
recovery is not school
it's real life
and you can't fake your way out of life
in real life, there's no teacher telling you what to do
your recovery is up to you
you make the choice now
but deciding to "drop out" is not an option
 there's no "dropping out" of recovery
because recovery,
recovery is life or death
what do you choose?

therapy was hard today, my therapist sat and listened to me, and he would say:

"it's brave of you to keep pushing through
when the darkness screams at you...

cry it out, let it out, don't hold back,
he told me I'm on the right track.

you're trying your best and that's what matters,
even when it feels like your heart is in shatters.

your depression is not who you are,
I believe in you and know you will go far.

it truly was the words I needed to hear,
it helped me realize that recovery is near."

- *recovery is possible and it is happening right in front of your eyes.*

listening to the next right thing on repeat
walking outside in the dark alone
watching the streetlights shine over the lake
the small water drops, so small at first
but a ripple effect grows
kind of like me
one small step
can ripple into something bigger
it's moments like this that reminds me
that life is worth it
I am worth it
and no matter how small I feel
I mean more than I'll ever know

each step means more than you'll ever know

hope doesn't always have to be this magical thing
sometimes, hope is simply getting out of bed
or eating a meal, when your eating disorder is telling you not to
hope is being honest about how you're really feeling, even if it's bad
hope is showing up to therapy and showing up for yourself
smiling is hope.
even crying is hope.
this poem is hope.
hope is holding on when you feel hopeless.
and by doing all these things,
you, yourself are hope.

I know you're tired. I can see it in your eyes. I know it feels like you need to be busy all the time to keep the tears inside, but I'm here to tell you that it's okay to cry. You don't need to run and hide. Just keep walking. Even if you're stumbling. Keep stumbling towards that light. You're going to be fine. I can promise you that. And I know you're exhausted of the same old routine, I know you're fighting every day to get out of bed and go on with your day, but I'm proud of you. Why? Because you keep showing up. You keep on going even when it feels like it's the hardest thing to do. I'm proud of you. Because you're you. And that in itself, is enough.

Maybe I did gain weight. But I also gained a year of memories with my nephew. I gained the opportunity to hold him and play with him.

Maybe I did gain weight. But I also gained 17 students who look up to me. I gained the opportunity to teach them and dance with them around the classroom.

Maybe I did gain weight. But I also gained a friend who will be there for me till the very end. I gained the opportunity to cry with her, laugh with her, and be myself around her.

Maybe I did gain weight. But I also gained a family, a classroom, and friends. I gained the opportunity to build a life with them by my side.

So yes, I did gain weight. But I also gained life.

And life is more important than any number will ever be.

PROTECTING THE INNER CHILD

"how dare you push me aside", she says

with shaky hands,

a speeding heart,

and those quick & shallow breaths.

"I'm not safe here", she says.

when I'm alone with nothing to fear.

"something is wrong", she says.

and she sends me into a panic attack.

my body remembers it all

from the feeling in my chest,

all the way to the soles of my feet.

my body shuts down.

it's frozen in time.

begging me to put her into safety,

I hold on to her tightly,

comfort her,

and reassure her,

"we're safe here, I promise"

-     the body keeps the score

mendED

What if I told you that the things that happened to you were not your fault?

The hate you've placed on your body is misplaced.

I know it's easier to blame your body,

because of the stories you've been told.

But how about you change the story?

Take the pen back and rewrite it.

Because the problem was never your body.

The problem was what they said about you,

And what you've said about yourself, as a result.

You have every right to be angry,

But don't put that anger out on your body,

When it's been on your team all along.

It was never you vs your body.

It was you and your body vs them.

- your body is fighting *for* you, not *against* you.

THIS FOG WON'T LAST FOREVER

I know sometimes it feels like your head is full of smoke and you can't see past it, but you don't have to go through this alone. Someone will be there to guide you and lend you a helping hand. Hold onto those people as they walk hand in hand with you until you find your way out of this fog. One day, you'll be able to see a clear path ahead. One day you'll be able to breathe again.

mendED

They told me to leave it all behind

So, I threw my old jeans away
They didn't fit me anymore
It was once full of promises
Those wicked and cruel promises
And so, I worked so hard, so f***ing hard,
to fit into those size █ jeans

But all it left me was
Pain and shame
It was nothing but a game

It was time to let go
Of those old, broken dreams
Leave behind those old, torn up jeans

So, I threw them away
They didn't fit me anymore
Now all that's left is an empty drawer

I'm so afraid of change
That I'm scared to let you go
After all, you were my safety blanket
A safety blanket I've outgrown
Living a life without you
Would be like starting over
Like the start of something new
Learning to live again
And breaking free from you
I'm on my own now
I've got to go my own way
So, I can live to see another day

A LETTER FROM MY BODY

To the girl who is in pain,

I get it, you're hurt
but now I am hurting, too
from your harsh behaviors.
you have cut me,
scarred me,
starved me,
beaten me alive,
when all I've done is try to keep you alive.
I don't know why you are taking your pain out on me.
I am not against you.
I am with you.
I have always been with you.
I am fighting for you to make it through this,
because what happened to you was not because of you,
or because of me.
it was not your fault,
and I want you to know,
that hurting me, is not the answer.
because hurting me only gives more power to them,
you can take that power back.
but I need you to take care of me,
as I am trying to take care of you.
I can't do this on my own.
we're on the same team here.

Sincerely,
your body

I'm hanging off the edge of a cliff
And I'm ready to let go
To give it all up
My hands are aching
My knees are scraping
And I'm struggling to breathe
A faint voice whispers in my mind
"Hold on, don't let go"
I clench the rocks a little tighter
My body aches in pain
But I grab onto the rope
That has been there all along
And I pull myself up
Step by step
And I make it to the top
The view is beautiful
The climb was painful
But it was worth it
I look out into the sky and think
I'm so glad I've arrived
I'm so glad I survived
I'm even glad that I'm alive

your eating disorder will romanticize itself as you continue this recovery journey.

he will remind you of how skinny you were, the compliments you received, the euphoria you felt from the (false) sense of control. he will tell you to come back to him. do not listen.

he will not remind you of the times he left you, breathless and lifeless, on the floor. he will not remind you of the times you couldn't sleep because your heart rate was a little too high. he will not remind you of the hunger pains, or the sounds your stomach made, or even the tears your family cried as they watched you deteriorate.

as recovery gets harder, he will blur out these truths and glorify the reality you lived in for so long.

once you begin to question recovery, he will beg for you to come back.

do not.

look him in the eyes and say, "not again".

because you were not happier.

you may have been smaller.

but you were not happier.

I'm recovering so I can hold my nephew and bounce up and down with him to make him smile. I'm recovering so I can teach a lesson without feeling faint and dizzy. I'm recovering so I can go out to eat with my friends. I'm recovering so I can graduate. I'm recovering so I can be there for my sister's wedding. I'm recovering because my dad didn't get the chance to. I'm recovering to make him proud. I'm recovering so the girls who bullied me no longer have power over me. I'm recovering for hope. I'm recovering for freedom. I'm recovering for possibility. I'm recovering so that anyone who is struggling knows that there is a way out.

I'm recovering for you. I'm recovering for me.

A DIFFERENT CINDERELLA STORY

I know you want someone to save you, to sweep you off your feet. A fairy god mother, perhaps, someone to take the pain away, even if it's just for one night. But I'm here to tell you to be your own fairy god mother. Be your own prince charming. It doesn't take one night, a sprinkle of magic dust, to make it all better. It will take time, lots of hard work. But one day you will wake up, look in the mirror, open the windows to sing, and put on your own glass slippers.

- my darling, you don't need saving. you're magic just as you are.

recovery is scary,

living a life with an eating disorder is even scarier.

resilient (adj.) | ability to withstand or recover quickly from difficult conditions

I am not resilient because I recovered quickly. I am not resilient because I was able to withstand. I broke down. more times than I can count. my recovery was not quick. it took me years to even want to recover. it took me years to begin to understand what recovery means. my resilience is not based on how quickly I was able to "recover". my resilience is not based on what I have withstood. my resilience is falling, falling hard but getting back up, scraped knees and all. my resilience is tears, lots of tears that I would not wipe away, because those tears remind me that I'm alive. my resilience is wanting to give up but choosing to keep going. my resilience is saying yes to recovery, no matter how long, how hard, and how painful it might be. my resilience is simply looking myself in the mirror and saying,

"I am resilient"

"your weight doesn't define your worth"

but the scale is staring at me
screaming at me to just take the step
and see what number I'm at.

"If you're at ███ pounds, you can eat a little more,
but if you're not, you'll eat less, and you'll be sure to get your work
outs in.
remember, I'm just here to keep you healthy and make sure you're
where you need to be"

I call bull****.

I've been down this road before. far too many times. where a number
dictates my choices, dictates my day. healthy to you is when I'm
buried in my grave. that's where you want me to be. and you want the
truth? sometimes, it sounds promising. and I start to believe you. the
urge is there. the urge is strong. I mean, it can't hurt to just take that
step and see that number one time, right? wrong. it does hurt. it hurts
my body, it hurts my loved ones, it hurts me. I'm not going down that
road again.

the scale is screaming at me
but I scream back
and instead of taking that step
I smash it

I hope you realize how brave you are to continue standing when everything around you is crashing down. I hope that no matter what happens, you continue to stand, because you are an indestructible force. You are powerful, even when you feel powerless. And when you find yourself on the ground, I hope you find the strength to pick yourself back up and stand again. Because you are strong. You are so strong. Take those bricks they threw at you and build a castle out of them. You are unstoppable and you are going to do amazing things. I hope that you can remember that. And I hope that when life gets you feeling like you can't take it anymore, that you decide to stay. That you decide to live. Because you deserve to.

You deserve to live.

I see you with those tired eyes, trying so hard to stay alive. I see you putting in so much work for others, and forgetting about your own needs. You help so much. Give everyone all you can offer. I wish you could do the same for yourself. Rest those tired eyes. I need you to be okay. I know how much you love others, I just wish you'd love yourself too.

Take a deep breath. Stay alive.

- a note to myself

A note to my readers:

My eating disorder took over my life. It was something I struggled with for so long, something I was so good at hiding. Until I couldn't hide it anymore. It was screaming at me and staring me in the eyes. I knew I couldn't keep living like this. And if I let the eating disorder continue to control me, it would soon take my life. After months and months of tears in therapy, calling my insurance, applying for treatment scholarships, hours of intake sessions, and looking into different treatment centers, I finally got the help that I needed. It was the hardest thing I ever had to do. Admitting I had an eating disorder was hard. Admitting that I couldn't do it on my own was even harder. But hard does not mean impossible.

I didn't choose an eating disorder, but I did choose recovery. And it's something I have to choose every day. Recovery is not linear, and by no means, was my healing process linear. One day I would have a poem in the "breaking" section, and the next day I'd have a poem in the "mending" section. One day, I'd be able to follow my meal plan and feel amazing. The next day, I cried at the sight of apple sauce. I slipped and fell, so many times. I fell hard. But I got back up every time and continued to put one foot in front of the other. I continued to do the next right thing.

Some people may ask why I'm so honest about this. Some people may say that my honesty only hinders my recovery, but I think the opposite. I think my honesty brings out who I really am. I think my honesty can help others.
So, **I will continue to recover and heal loudly. So not one more person suffers quietly.**

With that being said, if any of you are struggling, know you are not alone. You are worthy of love and the number on the scale does not define you. The food you eat does not define you. Your eating disorder does not define you. You are so much more than a body. You are so much than an eating disorder.

Recovery is possible. And it is happening every day.

RESOURCES

The scariest thing I did for myself was reach out for help, but it was also the most important thing I've done for myself. If I hadn't gotten help, I wouldn't have this book out today. I don't even know if I would be here today. So, if you are struggling in any way, please reach out for help and know that you are deserving of help. You are not a lost cause. You are not alone. You can beat this. Here is a list of resources where you can find treatment providers/treatment facilities, a screening tool, and numbers to contact if you are in need of extra support:

NATIONAL ALLIANCE FOR EATING DISORDERS
www.findEDhelp.com
info@allianceforeatingdisorders.com
866-662-1235

NATIONAL EATING DISORDER ASSOCIATION
www.nationaleatingdisorders.org/screening-tool
https://map.nationaleatingdisorders.org
800- 931-2237

NATIONAL ALLIANCE ON MENTAL ILLNESS
www.nami.org/help
800-950-6264

NATIONAL SUICIDE PREVENTION HOTLINE
www.suicidepreventionlifeline.org
800-273-8255

CRISIS TEXT LINE
Text NEDA to 741741

This is not an exhaustive list of resources by any means. Please reach out to a therapist or physician if more resources are needed.

BOOKS

Below are a list of books I have read in treatment that were most helpful for me. These books can serve as a resource for someone in recovery themselves, or someone who just wants to learn more about eating disorders. If you know someone who is struggling with an eating disorder, the best thing you can do for them is to listen to them, support them, and be there for them. By educating yourself on eating disorders, you are supporting them. And that means more to us than you will ever know. We are better when we recover together.

8 Keys to Recovery from an Eating Disorder - Carolyn Costin and Gwen Schubert Grabb

Eating in the Light of the Moon - Anita Johnson

Life Beyond Your Eating Disorder - Johanna Kandel

Life Without ED - Jenni Schaffer

Goodbye ED, Hello Me - Jenni Schaffer

The Inside Scoop on Eating Disorder Recovery - Jennifer Rollin and Colleen Reichmann

Sick Enough - Jennifer Gaudiani

ACKNOWLEDGEMENTS

Bear with me here as this is going to be the longest acknowledgements page you've ever read. If that doesn't show you how much I love my friends, then I don't know what will.

First and foremost, I want to thank everyone who took the time to read this. You are the reason I write. You are the reason I continue to fight. I know this book can be a lot to take in. I know it is sad. But, I hope it can bring some insight into the reality of eating disorders. I hope this serves as a reminder that you are never as alone as you think you are.

Mom, my dear mom. I don't know how I can possibly fit this into one short paragraph because I could write a whole other book on how much I love you and how grateful I am for you. First of all, thank you for giving me life and for protecting me. I always say this, but I truly mean it - you are the strongest woman I know. You have been through hell and back, but no matter what you were put through, you did everything you possibly could to make sure I was happy and loved. I love you to the moon and back.

Dad, there are tears streaming down my face as I write this acknowledgement because you're no longer here to read this, but I know that you are watching over me and I know you would be proud of me. You have always been a reason for me to recover, and I will do that for you. I am the person I am today because of you. You have taught me how to be strong and how to get up and keep on fighting, even when I get knocked down. Thank you for being here for me throughout this tough journey. Thank you for never giving up on me. Thank you for believing in me till your very last breath. I miss you. I miss you so much. (August 4th 1965-November 20th 2021)

Malissa, my beautiful little sister, who sometimes I forget is younger than me, thank you for finding me on the scale that one afternoon and questioning me - I would have never admitted I had a problem if it wasn't for you. Thank you for spoon feeding me when I couldn't get myself to eat. Thank you for catching me in my lies. And while you still get annoyed and frustrated with me, I appreciate you anyways. Even when it doesn't feel like it. I still remember the day you came in my room, crying because of how worried you were for me. That is when I knew I needed to recover. So, thank you for caring and for loving me unconditionally.

Katelynn, thank you for trying your best to educate me. I know I never listened to you. I know I got mad at you (I know I still do) but thank you for continuing to try anyways. Although we may never agree on some things, although we always seem to butt heads, I am so thankful that you're still here for me and that you love me always. You'll always be my favorite person to laugh with and party with.

To my Grandma Rita. I feel so lucky to have a grandma like you. Thanks for calling me every day while I was in treatment to see how I was doing. Thanks for cooking for me and for staying on the phone with me until I ate something. I know it's not the same, but I will do everything I can to live up to dad in his honor. I will recover so you can be proud, and so that he will be proud. Believe me when I say that you raised him to be as strong as he was. Now I will be strong.

To my best friend, Logan Davis. I can't imagine where I would be without you. You are one of the only people I know I can talk to without judgement. Thank you for that. Thank you for driving me to treatment, both times. Thank you for visiting me in treatment and for the letters you sent. Thank you for inspiring me to be my true self – regardless of what people think. You make me want to continue fighting for my recovery.

To my cousin, Kaminie. My soul sister. I remember FaceTiming you whenever I was struggling with behaviors, and you'd sit with me until the urge passed. I don't think you knew how helpful that was for me, but I'm telling you now. I appreciate your support so much. From giving me recipes to researching and spreading awareness on eating disorders. You are going to be an amazing dietitian and I'm so excited to see how many people you help along the way.

To my Swiftie Storm Sister, Natalia. You were one of the first people I confided in about my struggles with eating. Thank you for hyping me up when I finished a meal. Thank you for texting me to hold me accountable with my meal plan. Thank you for sending me Taylor Swift content when I needed a smile. I thank Taylor Swift every day for bringing someone as amazing as you into my life. I love you to the moon and to Saturn, forever and always.

To my best friend, Márcia, who just so happens to live 4,000 miles away from me. Distance means nothing when someone means so much. From day one, I knew you'd be someone so important to me. I don't know when the day will come when I get to hug you and meet you in person, but then again, it gives me another reason to recover. I love you endlessly, the Monica to my Rachel. I'll be there for you, cause you're there for me too.

To my mentor, Angela Hollenback. Opening up to you about my eating disorder was one of the hardest things I've done, but it was also one of the best things I have ever done for myself. You have been so much more than just a mentor, Angela. You have become a lifelong friend. Thank you for allowing me to cry on your shoulder. Thank you for the daily accountability texts. Thank you for letting me FaceTime you when I'm in the middle of a mental break down. You are the person who never fails to remind me of what I am recovering for.

To my therapist, Dr. Mitchell. I don't even know where to begin. I still remember the day I told you about my eating disorder. You were the one provider who didn't look at me differently. From day one, you did everything you could to support me. By setting goals with me, sitting with me as I cried, writing me recommendations for treatment scholarships, researching treatment options, and giving me a safe space to just be. There are not enough words to describe how thankful I am for you and everything you continue to do for me. Thank you for caring about me, thank you for believing in me, thank you for encouraging me, thank you for never giving up on me, and most importantly, thank you for seeing me as Ashley. You mean the world to me, Dr. Mitchell, and when I say you saved my life, I mean it. I really do.

To the Alliance for ED Awareness and Johanna Kandel. At a time when I felt broken, confused, and alone, you reminded me that I am far from alone, and that there is a whole community of people who have been through it themselves and are rooting for me and my recovery. I truly don't know if I would've gone into treatment and gotten the help I needed if it wasn't for this amazing organization. Johanna, thank you for your honesty and your bravery to share your story and build this life-saving organization. You are an inspiration.

To my precious nephew, Izeyah. I know you aren't old enough to even walk yet, but I'm writing this to you anyways, so that when you're older, you will know just what you've done for me. I was in treatment on my birthday, when my sister called me to tell me she was pregnant with you. From that day forward, I made it my mission to recover. I was in treatment, again, when you were first born. It broke my heart to miss that special moment. It is now my mission to not miss any more of these precious moments in your life. I am so blessed to be your Auntie Ashley.

To my Uncle George for being someone that I look up to and for always helping me out in my recovery, whether that is financially or just through your support. You are the funniest person I know but also one of the most amazing guys that I know. I wish I could repay you for all you have done for me.

To my treatment friends, whether I met you in residential, PHP, IOP, or through the Alliance, you all mean more to me than you'll ever know. I started treatment with the thought that I was a burden to everyone. I left treatment knowing that I could impact people's lives, even if it's just one person. There's too many people to name in this section, but you know who you are. My sister warriors. Keep fighting.

To anyone who's name I didn't have the space to write. I love you guys. For everything. Thank you for helping me grow into the person I am today.

And last but not least, to Taylor Swift, the singer/songwriter who probably has no idea I exist and who just so happens to get her own page in my book. If you know me, then you know that this book wouldn't be right if I didn't thank Taylor in some way.

So, Taylor Swift, thank you. Thank you from the bottom of my heart. Your vulnerability in Miss Americana helped me come to terms with and accept my eating disorder for what it is – an eating disorder. Thank you for helping me believe that whispers behind my back do not define me and that I am the person who survived a bunch of rainstorms and kept walking. Thank you for helping me become "clean". I'll meet you someday. And until then, I'll have another reason to recover.

Printed in Great Britain
by Amazon

27034127R00066